This journal belongs to:

____

Made in the USA
Las Vegas, NV
27 November 2021

35421222R00070